DON'T TELL
WORK (AND

POCKET LIBRARIES
NOT FOR RESALE

DON'T TELL DICK JOKES AT WORK (AND OTHER TIPS)

How Any Man Can Confidently Foster a Safe Workplace for Women

By J. A. Davids

Bulk Purchases: Enterprise and educational organizations are eligible for wholesale pricing. Contact the publisher at talkhumantome@gmail.com for details.

Written in Boston, Massachusetts. Published in Seattle, Washington.

1. Work Environment. 2. Diversity and Leadership 3. Business Etiquette. 4. Career Development.

ISBN-13: 978-0-9896632-3-6

*For the men brave enough to help
women embrace their potential.*

Dear Men,

You are nice. I'm sure that you already know the Golden Rule: treat others as you would like to be treated. Even so, you may struggle with how to help women feel more welcome in the workplace.

I interviewed women and men in tech, and I read extensively on the topic of gender and tech culture. Then, I converted my research into lessons that will equip you with practical, actionable ways to achieve a work culture that appeals to both women and men.

Embody the following lessons, and I promise that you will avoid confusion and frustration at the office, and will come to know many women who are delighted to call you their colleague.

Sincerely,
J. A. Davids

Table of Contents

INTRODUCTION

I wrote this book to help men in male-dominated work environments welcome and recruit women to their teams.

Anyone can play an important part in creating a more welcoming work environment. After reading this book, you will be able to:

- Minimize gender-specific communication issues.
- Identify what to do *today* to attract and retain female hires in the upcoming weeks.
- Recognize, reduce, and prevent inappropriate behavior by men on your team.
- Develop a list of specific actions to make your organization an amazing place for women to work.
- Relate better to women's experiences at work, which will help you become a well-respected leader of men and women alike.

Book Structure

The book is laid out in two parts. "Part One" provides an overview of challenges women have faced – and continue to face – in the US workforce. The section includes research about the history of women in the US workforce, as well as exclusive interviews and survey results.

"Part Two" delivers ten specific lessons about how you can improve your workplace for women. Each lesson is composed of the following elements:

- "The Challenge": Introduces you to a specific challenge that men might face when trying to welcome women at work.
- "Empathy Session": This fictional story will immerse you in a hypothetical version of "The Challenge."
- "Question": A pointed question will help you develop your own position on the "Empathy Session."

- "Facts To Know": This section presents reference material that is relevant to "The Challenge."
- "Action Items": A detailed list of actions helps you form a plan to address "The Challenge" at your own workplace.

Questions

Early readers of the book have frequently returned to me with questions specific to their own lives. For example, "I had a meeting with a woman and I said, 'X, Y, and Z.'" Is that okay to do?" That's great because it means readers like you are fully engaging with the lessons and looking to connect these lessons with your own lives.

As you read the book, write down any questions that arise for you. If you don't find the answers to those questions after reading this book in its entirety, please submit your own question(s) by emailing talkhumantome@gmail.com. I will make every attempt to answer your question(s).

Reference Links

Throughout the book, I provide links to supplemental online information that will enrich your experience. Visit www.juliadavids.com/book-links to easily navigate to all of the links from the book.

PART I: THE PROBLEM

A RECENT HISTORY OF WORKING WOMEN IN THE UNITED STATES

The United States government has a history of educating men about how to recruit and welcome women to the workplace. In 1943, for example, the US War Department published a pamphlet of tips called "You're Going to Employ Women."

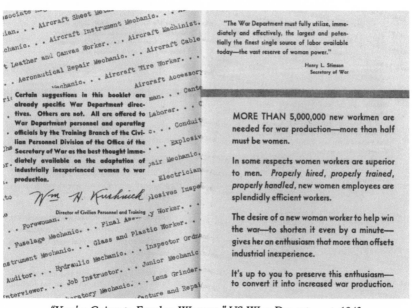

"You're Going to Employ Women." US War Department. 1943.

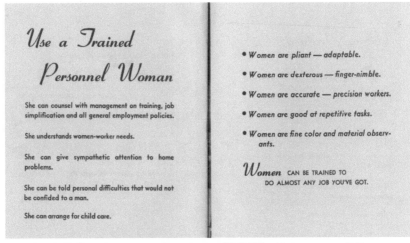

Use a Trained Personnel Woman

She can counsel with management on training, job simplification and all general employment policies.

She understands women-worker needs.

She can give sympathetic attention to home problems.

She can be told personal difficulties that would not be confided to a man.

She can arrange for child care.

* Women are pliant — adaptable.

* Women are dexterous — finger-nimble.

* Women are accurate — precision workers.

* Women are good at repetitive tasks.

* Women are fine color and material observants.

Women CAN BE TRAINED TO DO ALMOST ANY JOB YOU'VE GOT.

"You're Going to Employ Women." US War Department. 1943.

The pamphlet contains a variety of practical tips. The publication describes women's abilities and needs in regard to work. I agree with the sentiment that our country should utilize our "vast reserve of woman power." I also agree that "women can be trained to do almost any job you've got." (Although I'd remove the "almost.") However, much of the advice describes women in an outdated fashion.

Much has improved for women in the workplace since the publication of this wartime pamphlet. A quick read of the fact sheet "12 Stats About Working Women" produced by the Department of Labor happily reveals that "women's participation in the US labor force has climbed since WWII: from 32.7 percent in 1948 to 56.8 percent in 2016."[1,2] Additionally, "the range of occupations women workers hold has also expanded, with women making notable gains in professional and managerial occupations. In 2016, more than one in three lawyers was a woman compared to fewer than 1 in 10 in 1974."

Yet today, certain industries have not yet heeded the emphatic and practical message: "You're Going To Employ Women."

Certain industries chronically employ fewer women than men. The Women's Bureau, a branch of the US Department of Labor, tracks the number of women employed in each occupation.[3] Their analysis helps us identify which industries are least likely to employ women and most likely to employ men.

---

[1] bit.ly/2vTZbzE
[2] bit.ly/2L30Zen
[3] bit.ly/2nNRExC

Women account for less than 20 percent of the workforce in the following occupations: laborers; freight, stock, and material movers; software developers of applications and systems software; first-line supervisors of production and operating workers; and police and sheriff's patrol officers.

Women account for less than 10 percent of the workforce in the following occupations: grounds maintenance workers; sales workers; and truck drivers.

Women account for less than 5 percent of the workforce in the following occupations: construction laborers; carpenters; automotive service technicians and mechanics; and electricians.

Engineering fields continue to educate and employ women at a lower rate than men year over year.

WOMEN'S EMPLOYMENT IN STEM

As of 2011, just 13% of engineers were women, according to the U.S. Census Bureau.

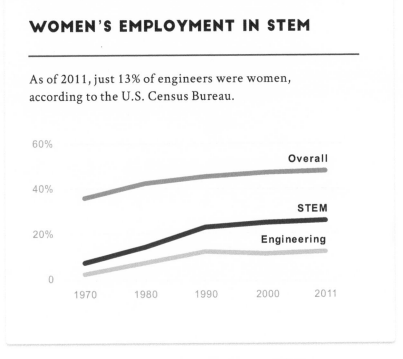

Chart 1. Women's Employment in STEM.

These equal employment challenges have earned STEM (Science, Technology, Engineering, and Mathematics fields) numerous appearances in news and pop culture. The employment gap truly is as dramatic as the latest Hollywood movie about the topic. As of 2011, just 13% of engineers were women, according to the US Census Bureau (see Chart 1).[4]

---

[4] bit.ly/2Pk9Lbl

STEM GENDER IMBALANCE

The gender imbalance becomes more severe as one moves from university to the workforce.

DEGREES
STEM Graduates in 2011

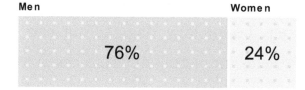

Men	Women
61%	39%

WORKFORCE
STEM Workforce in 2011

Men	Women
76%	24%

Chart 2. STEM Gender Imbalance.

The gender imbalance becomes more severe as one moves from university to the workforce. There is a significant difference between the number of women who graduate with STEM degrees and the number of women who continue to work in STEM fields. In 2011, the US Census Bureau found that 39% of women graduated with a science or engineering bachelor's degree; less than two thirds of women with this degree type were actively employed in the STEM workforce (see Chart 2).

Regardless of industry, women and men in the US are not afforded equal opportunity to hold senior, strategic business roles. Women simply hold far fewer leadership positions than men.

A 2017 article by the Center for American Progress (CAP) discusses the gap in women's leadership in the nation's top-performing companies:

> "While they are 44 percent of the overall S&P 500 labor force and 36 percent of first- or mid-level officials and managers in those companies, they are only 25 percent of executive- and senior-level officials and managers, hold only

20 percent of board seats, and are only 6 percent of CEOs." [5]

The same CAP article highlights the scarcity of women leaders in high-tech industries:

"In 2014, women were just 20 percent of executives, senior officers, and management in US high-tech industries. As recently as 2016, 43 percent of the 150 highest-earning public companies in Silicon Valley had no female executive officers at all."

Overall, the US workforce has come a long way in terms of employing women. However, there are clear areas for improvement in terms of employing women on equal terms with men. To achieve parity, certain industries, like STEM, should focus on hiring and retaining women in their workforce. Additionally, all fields would do well to increase the number of women holding leadership positions.

---

[5] ampr.gs/2q3TLRN

THE IMPACT OF GENDER IMBALANCE ON THE WORK ENVIRONMENT

I surveyed men and women who work in the tech industry and asked them to describe times when they *did* and *did not* fit in at work. I found that, overall, women and men described remarkably different experiences. Rather than tell you about these differences, I will provide the original responses so that you can discover them for yourself.

Read the responses with a critical eye, and consider the following questions:

- How do men and women differ in their description of fitting in?
- How do men and women adjust their behavior to fit in more at work?

Survey Prompt One

Describe a time when you *did not* fit in.

Man 1

Rarely

Man 2

Always. The challenge is to continually re-establish one's "fit" or place.

Man 3

This happened during my senior design course [in college]. I ended up working with three other guys. When I first met the team, I felt like a complete outsider. My group members where all tall white dudes who were on the school swim team... The early dynamic was strange. I think it was difficult for us to have a casual conversation. They were already friends and I was just getting to know them...

However, as we spent more time working together, a lot of the ice was broken. Above all else, we worked well together, even though we did not share much on the personal side. We did a good job of defining our roles within the team and establishing goals. This ended up being one of the best group experiences I ever had.

Man 4

I spent the last 10 years making fine art and music. Never been a full "nerd" and always felt like I should be able to fit in better—like I should buy miniatures or lolcat t-shirts or something. Always embarrassed to bring up philosophical or art historical points in conversations about games.

Man 5

[No response given to this question.]

Woman 1

Not that I did not fit in, but I definitely notice a different dynamic when I have a meeting and all the attendees are males. My company is really good with gender diversity so that's a rare occasion. So when it happens, I notice.

Woman 2

Constantly? I never feel like I fit in at work. The time I felt most alienated at work was when I came back from a month-long trip to our Chinese manufacturer and on the whiteboard it said "ultimate man competition," and two of my co-workers each had ticks by their name. There was a quote written directly under it quoting a third co-worker who said "I need some multiball action." I've never heard this co-worker talk about pinball. When I'm at work I try to nudge people to be more thoughtful and diversity-conscious (to my professional detriment), and clearly that had slipped wildly in the month I wasn't in the office. A week later, one of my co-workers carefully removed a single sticker and said that should count for a point in the man competition because he did it so well. I had been removing stickers all day and no one noticed or cared. In my current and previous jobs I've worked exclusively with all cis white men.

Woman 3

I spent seven years at a design consultancy firm, where all five principals were white, heterosexual, male, and over the age of 50. The two associates (including myself) were younger women of color.

Although I did excellent work, I never fit in entirely, although my differences were sometimes exploited as assets. For example, whenever my status as a millennial was advantageous with a particular client.

Being a woman put my promotion to principal out of reach. I know this because shortly before leaving the company, I had a frank conversation with the company president who made it clear that gender bias was not, and would not be, a topic of discussion in our workplace.

Woman 4

When people think I'm an intern on a job site I'm running because I'm a young (26 year old) woman.

When I'm the only woman in the room and someone makes a sexist joke and I'm the only person who doesn't laugh. When I'm treated with far less respect than my male colleagues.

Woman 5

I have been the only woman on engineering teams, and often the only woman in an office or entire building, for most of my career. Getting by meant being "one of the guys" or "den mother," neither of which comes naturally to me.

Socially, I was pushed into roles that don't suit me, usually by the way male colleagues treated me. The "one of the guys" expectation (which I could never truly be) meant things like being asked to participate in Fantasy Football, or being OK with commentary on "hot women" in video games, etc. The "den mother" expectation showed through with queries to defuse or decide arguments, provide food, calm a hot-tempered male developer, etc.

Survey Prompt Two

Describe a time when you *really* fit in.

Man 1

There was a perfect alignment of culture between co-workers and a genuine belief in the cause of the brand.

Man 2

When I'm reviewing code written by others, because I'm good at it, and I am very confident in my level of experience.

Man 3

I fit best on a "balanced team" that we'd created around a mobile technology product. I was leading the design and working with an engineer, tester, and product manager. Each of us had a clear idea of the outcome we were looking for, and could query each other for help directly, or help to find the support we needed. It was a respectful and self-directed experience. We worked together as equals.

Man 4

Most of the time.

Man 5

When "job" (specific task) requirements, and expectations "fit" with my offerings and potential contributions.

Woman 1

I've worked for 9 years at 3 different places and the only times I've felt like I fit in were when I faked interest in things my co-workers cared about. I can't say there was ever one day where I felt like I truly fit in.

Woman 2

In social settings where people can forget about age and hierarchy.

Woman 3

There was a scotch tasting happening in our lounge with about 10 men. I joined and tasted some great scotch, wondering why other women weren't joining.

Woman 4

I don't think I ever have. I left big tech companies to become self-employed five months ago, and now I feel like I finally fit in, but that's because I work alone and mostly telecommute. It's a tremendous relief to just be able to be myself, by myself.

Woman 5

There was one principal at my workplace who was my ally, mentor, and advocate. Whenever I worked with him, I felt valued and that my contributions were taken seriously. He was open-minded, endlessly curious, and our personalities meshed well. I think our relationship was based on mutual respect, and that's why it worked so well. When we had projects together, I never felt out of place.

WOMEN'S EXPERIENCES IN MALE-DOMINATED WORKPLACES

If you're wondering what it's like to build a career as a woman in a male-dominated workplace, there has never been a better time to find out. Online writing platforms provide a voice to women and allow you to access a colorful mosaic of impactful personal narratives.

A standout example is Susan Fowler's blog post "Reflecting On One Very, Very Strange Year At Uber," which illustrates the very worst frustrations that women might encounter while working in tech.[6] Fowler describes the unwelcoming culture that she encountered at Uber; the steps she took to resolve the issues; and her ultimate inability to resolve these issues due to the organization's cultural environment.

---

[6] bit.ly/2lRQlxv

To describe the typical challenges women face in their career in a male-dominated field, I've written a fictional story of one woman's career. (The following story is for illustration purposes and not representative of all women.)

The Hunter

You are a recent graduate who has spent two months looking for a job in tech. While the men in your class have all received several interviews and a few offers, you have only heard back from one company. That company didn't invite you to a technical interview. You met with a few men to talk about the work culture they were looking for, and to see if you were a "good fit."

You are convinced that you could demonstrate strong technical abilities if the opportunity to undergo a technical exercise were offered to you. But for now, you haven't had the chance to prove yourself, much less have the benefit of the doubt.

The Outsider

You worry about standing out as the "new one" at work and bringing unwanted attention to yourself. Your personal interests and lifestyle choices are different from those of others on your team. In their spare time, they like to play strategic board games on rainy days, and frisbee on sunny ones; you prefer to sew for a bit after putting your kids to bed. From the first day, you worry that the differences in your interests outside of work may impact your ability to connect with colleagues. You overhear someone mention that you are hard-to-read and a bit off-putting.

The Doubted

A few weeks into your new job, you head to the bar with your teammates. You feel like you are finally settling in with the guys. On the way back from the toilet, you overhear a team member question the strength of your professional qualifications, then a round of laughter.

You start to second-guess yourself, and wonder if you're really up to par. Were you only hired to fill a seat so recruiting could end for the year?

The Overlooked

As time passes, you start to notice that others rarely acknowledge your ideas. At first you deny the suspicion, but the facts keep piling up. Your proposals and initiatives receive less support than those of your other colleagues.

Now, you actively avoid offering your opinions. You don't make the extra effort to propose risky or experimental projects, because it just wouldn't pay off.

The Therapist

Co-workers regularly approach you about their own problems, as you have a reputation for being a good listener. Because of this, however, you find it difficult to focus on your own project. This week, you produced much less work than you had planned to produce.

A MAN'S EXPERIENCE IN MALE-DOMINATED WORKPLACES

Most narratives about issues that arise in male-dominated workplaces focus on women's experiences. When this happens, men often lose out on an opportunity to share their own experiences.

In 2016, I was eating at a restaurant and got to know the person sitting at the table next to mine. We got to talking. His vocation came up and so did the topic of my research. He kindly accepted my request to further discuss the issue of gender imbalance in tech. A few weeks later, we connected via phone for an interview.

In the interview, transcribed below, he describes the dynamics and challenges of working in a "Boys Club." While you read the interview transcript, note how the interviewee respects his women co-workers and is very aware of gender bias. At the same time, he is occasionally uncertain how to improve overall workplace communication between men and women.

While reading the transcript, try to answer the following questions:

- How would you describe the interviewee's general attitude toward the "Boys Club"?
- How do communication issues impact the interviewee's experience at work?

Interview Transcript

Name: [name withheld]

Employer: [top tech company; name withheld]

Date: 2016

Start by introducing yourself, including what you do day-to-day at work.

I am [name withheld]. I am a production engineer at [employer withheld]. I help keep the computers going.

Could you describe how well you feel that you fit in with your work group?

I feel like I fit in pretty well. As far as a crowd of, you know, geeks—geeks are pretty mainstream within that sub-demographic.

How does that make you feel?

Comfort and ease with being in a Boys Club. You have a whole bunch of stuff you don't have to think about or worry about, typically, if it's just boys. And so, just like when you're out with your friends and not around your kids, maybe you cuss more. The difference between [how I'd act outside of work and at] the workplace was literally zero. A thing which I've had a number of times.

The first woman, or any woman, is substantial. And it's not substantial in some sort of, guys are having to hold themselves back. It's just, it changes the dynamic completely. And there absolutely is stuff you're not going to say or stuff you're gonna say differently. Assuming that everybody there is in that portion of people who don't have a problem with women being around. You know, [men] who are relatively neutral.

Could you say a little more about the comfort of being in a "Boys Club"? And the shift of the first woman?

I can remember in an early job of mine, back in the mid-90s, I built an ISP, an Internet Service Provider. I was a technical lead, I wasn't really a manager, but I was still hiring people, because I was the lead technical person. And I had a technical support person who was a woman, [*withheld*], and I remember her well. I think I was completely oblivious to gender politics, at that point. It was a fairly small place, and the extent of that Boys Club, and everybody who was participating, it wasn't exclusivity, it was more just a friend pool.

So when she was added to the mix, I think there were a couple of moments where she was like, "Well, you know maybe that isn't the right kind of talk for work?" It's been a long, long time. But really, nobody was bent out of shape about that, and no problem.

So you guys would say something, and she would immediately talk to you then and there?

She is also a confident, self-aware person. This wasn't a big challenge for her. Because it wasn't sexism, so much as maybe just not-safe-for-work talk. It might have been extreme. In this case, in my personal experience, she was capable.

And the challenges she faced in that group were mild, and the challenges the group faced were mild as well. In this particular case, there wasn't anybody who worked there who had any desire to limit or talk down to someone because of their gender.

A place that I worked at in the late 90s that had a Boys Club was definitely resistant to hiring women simply based on merit. They had a strong, what they would call, cultural bias, which, based on results over time, I began to suspect involved being a Boys Club.

So this Boys Club. How did you pick up on that? What signaled that this was a Boys Club, besides, perhaps, the fact that there were only boys in the club?

So in the Software Engineering department, there were women who were hired, but...uhh...it's hard to distinguish. You have a bunch of bright, cocky software engineers. It's hard to distinguish elitism from sexism sometimes. So, you know, you're bright, you know what you're doing, you don't have a lot of time or patience for someone who doesn't. Man or woman.

You know, it's not an attitude I approve of anyways. But, you know, you have people who are already like that. And then you introduce a non-senior position, who is also a woman, and you observe that she gets a lot of dirty work.

You feel like you've observed someone who was hired, but is still an outsider. And I didn't really see that with the guys. I don't know how instructive that is, but I would say that what I observed, I ultimately categorized as gender-oriented, encouraged by an elite club attitude. To me, the men pretty clearly acted out with more strength because the person on the receiving end was a woman and wasn't one of the cool kids. Gender was a simple part of that.

How do you see this sort of club manifest itself today in your work?

We hire women. There are women all over the place at [*Employer Withheld*]. Most teams, after they reach a certain size... by the time you have ten people on your team, there's a pretty good chance that there's gonna be a woman on the team.

There's still a lot of men. But it's rarely allowed to be a Boys Club, except when you're only getting with your smallest, most immediate team. You're almost always going to be involved with larger teams, other groups, that are going to have both genders.

MEN UNSURE HOW TO SUPPORT WOMEN IN MALE-DOMINATED WORKPLACES

If you're reading this book, you probably try to embody civil, good, and generous treatment of people, no matter their sex or gender.

After reading about how women feel less welcome in male-dominated workplaces, you probably want to help support them at work.

But you might be uncertain about exactly how to go about supporting women at work. If that sounds like you, you aren't alone.

Recently, I asked men in my professional LinkedIn network to describe what they have done in the past to help a female colleague feel more welcome at work. Over 4,000 people read this LinkedIn post, demonstrating clear interest in the topic. And I received a few truly inspiring responses from men.

One man messaged me on LinkedIn to say that he loved the mission of welcoming women at work, especially in light of his daughter's future career. That said, he was puzzled as to how to begin:

"I hope that I have done things to make my female colleagues feel more welcome over the course of my career, but I'm not recalling any specific or compelling stories...need to do a little digging or perhaps make even more of an effort!

As the father of a young daughter who I would like to see pursue any career she chooses, I would hope that her male colleagues would take this effort regardless of the industry that she is in."

— Male Software Marketer

"It's a man's industry. It has been for 150 years. It's crazy.

My female co-worker and I share an office. I have seen a bit from her perspective. And I see how she's treated in meetings. Over the past two years she's been fighting to prove herself. With the guys, they accept you and give you information. For the women, they have to continually ask for help. That's super frustrating.

If you're not looking for it, it's easy to miss... I didn't know the word "mansplaining" before I worked for the railroad.

My manager and co-manager are both female. I can see the guys constantly interrupting them. They both now get invited to important meetings. I can see they have respect and are working for it.

(continued)

The ways I feel like I can support them is to be aware of it. I take opportunities to remind people that they can talk to them, because they know the answers, that is their purview.

Things happen so fast. For the women, if something is said or done, they are immediately aware of it. It takes longer for me to notice and empathize. I'd like to get quicker at being able to recognize it. Whereas they can notice it [immediately and] be like 'eff you.' If the same thing gets said to me, I don't feel like it's malicious.

I work with these women a lot. I spend 40-50 hours a week with them. We're basically dating. I know they're very knowledgeable and talented. But how do I communicate that to other people in other departments? How do I speak for them?"

— Public Transit Employee

Another man openly described how he works in "a man's industry" and sees that women he works with have struggled to build credibility. He has taken some actions to support these women, but he is uncertain if he is headed in the right direction.

If you're reading this book, it's likely that *you*, just like these men, respect women and earnestly want to make sure women feel welcome. But...you don't know how to start or how to improve.

The remainder of this book is dedicated to explaining the exact actions you can take to support women colleagues. In the following chapters, *you* will learn how to identify opportunities to build bridges and ensure women feel welcome in the workplace. This book will inject clarity and context into statements and advice from women like:

- "I am equal, capable, and strong."
- "I am not 'aggressive' or 'sensitive' or 'controlling.'"

- "A company should have a professional atmosphere. Act professionally around women, as well as around men."
- "Speak professionally, without profanities or sexual innuendos."
- "Consider whether your actions contribute to the organization's goals."

You don't have to wait for a corporate diversity and culture improvement initiative. You don't need a committee, a stakeholder meeting, or a budget. You certainly don't need executive approval.

All you need is an open mind and a sincere desire to make things better. Let's go!

PART 2: THE SOLUTION

TIP 1: REFINE RECRUITING PRACTICES

The Challenge

Some employers claim that it is difficult to find qualified women candidates to interview and hire. I believe that there are enough women candidates qualified to fill the toughest of roles.

Then why does there appear to be a shortage of women to hire? First, women aren't invited for as many first-round interviews because employers and recruiters are subconsciously biased against women. Second, employers often dismiss women that do get invited for onsite interviews as not being the right "cultural fit."

These two factors lead to a perceived lack of qualified women applicants. In turn, this *perceived* lack becomes a *real* lack.

Empathy Session

Emily needs to recruit for a position on her engineering team, which has three men and no women. She would like to achieve a more gender-balanced team, but her past recruiting efforts haven't yielded promising women candidates.

Question

How should she adjust her hiring plans so that she can meet her interview goal?

Facts To Know

Women often self-select out of applying to jobs where they don't meet the full skill set or experience level, while men don't. For more information, read this 2014 article by Harvard Business Review: "Why Women Don't Apply for Jobs Unless They're 100% Qualified."[7]

---

[7] bit.ly/2qtTwj2

Researchers have noted that men are more likely to be hired—and promoted—for potential, while women are more likely to be hired for existing skills. Read the 2014 article "How The 'New Discrimination' Is Holding Women Back" to learn more.[8]

Mini Tip   **Reference Links Available**
Remember that you can visit www.juliadavids.com/book-links to easily navigate to all of the links in this book.

Actions

Remember your goal is to hire strong employees, not friends.

- "Cultural fit" too often gets conflated with "reminds me of a friend." The more men who

---

[8] bit.ly/2KYP5lK

work at an organization, the more that these men will foster a culture that finds itself appealing to male, rather than female, applicants. As such, fewer and fewer women will be deemed "cultural fits."

- Consider freezing referral hiring bonuses, through which employees are paid to refer their friends. While hiring friends may promote a more fraternal workplace, it could deprive your company of opportunities to grow more diverse.

Know that women candidates actively seek work environments that support them. To see how women evaluate work environments for gender equality and welcomeness towards women, you can read job boards that support their needs.

- Tech Ladies connects women in tech with jobs in tech.[9]
- InHerSight encourages women to rate businesses based on how women-friendly they

---

[9] hiretechladies.com

are, and matches women with employers.[10] For example, the following is the profile page for Vice Media:

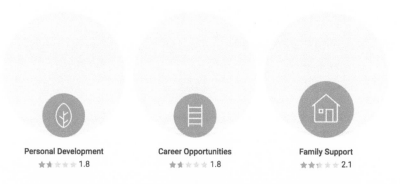

INHERSIGHT SCORE

2.0

★★☆☆☆

Personal Development	Career Opportunities	Family Support
★★☆☆☆ 1.8	★★☆☆☆ 1.8	★★☆☆☆ 2.1

---

[10] inhersight.com

Social Activities and Environment	3.4	
Paid Time Off	2.8	
Maternity and Adoptive Leave	2.4	
Management Opportunities for Women	2.3	
Family Growth Support	2.2	
Ability to Telecommute	2.2	
The People You Work With	1.8	
Equal Opportunities for Women and Men	1.7	
Female Representation in Top Leadership	1.7	
Salary Satisfaction	1.7	
Learning Opportunities	1.6	
Flexible Work Hours	1.5	
Wellness Initiatives	1.5	
Sponsorship or Mentorship Program	1.2	
Employer Responsiveness	N/A	

Document the ratio of women to men at your organization, and among candidates who you consider for an open position.

- Note which type of team women tend to join (e.g., engineering, sales, marketing) and the number of women who hold leadership positions in your company.
- Update this record month-to-month.
- You might even evaluate the number of women who act as advisors and investors.

Get familiar with your own biases.

- Project Implicit has created a method for assessing your implicit, subconscious, associations between concepts.[11] For example, you can test if you associate women more strongly with the concept of "family" than "career." Or you can measure if you associate women more strongly with the concept of "liberal arts" than "science."

- To test your biases, visit Project Implicit's test bank online.[12] You may be surprised by the results.

---

[11] implicit.harvard.edu
[12] bit.ly/1m808ph

Implicit Association Test

Next, you will use the 'E' and 'I' computer keys to categorize items into groups as fast as you can. These are the four groups and the items that belong to each:

Category	Items
Male	Ben, Paul, Daniel, John, Jeffrey
Female	Rebecca, Michelle, Emily, Julia, Anna
Career	Career, Corporation, Salary, Office, Professional, Management, Business
Family	Wedding, Marriage, Parents, Relatives, Family, Home, Children

There are seven parts. The instructions change for each part. Pay attention!

Continue

· Project Implicit ·

Preview of Project Implicit's Gender – Career IAT

Guard yourself against gender bias in hiring decisions.

- Consider reviewing résumés or applications name-blind.

- Articulate to yourself and to your team whether you are hiring for potential or for current skills.

- Measure candidates against one another by assigning all of them the same exercise. Their performance on this exercise can supplement the résumé and in-person interview.

Attract more applications from women.

- Adjust absolute requirements in job descriptions. For example, it's possible that one must not fit 100% of the "Required Skills" to be considered a promising candidate.

- To evaluate the gender-neutral appeal of your business writing, such as job postings and culture descriptions, use a service like Textio.[13] The service highlights words likely to appeal to men or women, and rates the entire text sample on a scale of "highly masculine" to "highly feminine." To demonstrate how the service works, I copied text from an UberEats job post and pasted it into Textio. The results are shown below.

---

[13] textio.com

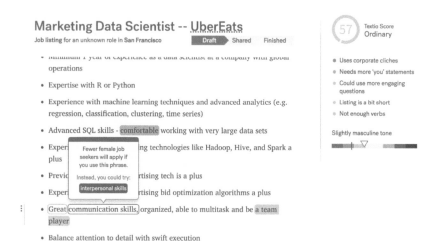

Revise your company's culture or mission descriptions, which may be promoted on your company's Team page.

- It's likely that your company values individuality, but descriptions that emphasize nerd-hood and beer nights could be off-putting to brilliant women candidates. A work-all-night, Soylent-all-day attitude might have been critical to start a company, but your workplace will need some wholesome culture shifts as it grows up.

Craft and publish a diversity policy.

- Learn from large companies with huge budgets and departments dedicated to producing recruiting guidelines. For example, take a look at Microsoft's strong "Diversity and Inclusion" website.[14] That said, even with many resources dedicated to this issue, companies like Microsoft still have work to do. In 2016, Gwen Houston, Chief Diversity & Inclusion Officer at Microsoft, noted that only "33.6 percent of [technical and non-technical] employees who joined the company directly from college were women." In this statement, Houston does not specifically outline a concrete plan to have 50% women and 50% men in the incoming pipeline of new university hires.[15]

- Write out concrete diversity hiring and employment goals based on what makes sense for your team and company.

- Propose steps that your company or your team can take to meet those goals.

---

[14] bit.ly/2w89D5S
[15] bit.ly/2FeQ7sI

- Acknowledge that you may need to look wider and longer to find women candidates for certain roles.
- Energize and educate others about this initiative.

Increase the number of the women leaders in your life, even if you don't have any at your own organization.

- Follow prominent women in your field on LinkedIn and Twitter to expose yourself to strong women with voices and opinions on business-critical topics.
- When these women share compelling articles or statements on their social networks, share them on your own social network. In this way, you will find yourself naturally promoting a more evenly gendered mix of opinions.

Expand the diversity of your professional acquaintances and your friend group. Having a larger pool of social and professional connections will naturally influence your conception of who is qualified or who may be a good culture fit for your company.

- Go to meetups or groups in your professional domain to introduce yourself to women and a diversity of other individuals. You can find informal and formal interest groups at Meetup, especially in large cities.[16] You can also attend special interest conferences in your field.

- At these community events, make acquaintance with women. Strike up conversations with people who you do not find yourself eager to approach, and invite sharp and compelling women to apply for relevant open positions at your company.

---

[16] meetup.com

TIP 2: UNDERSTAND WORK-APPROPRIATE CONVERSATION

The Challenge

Discovering more about your co-workers helps you bond with them. People are naturally curious and inquisitive, so it's totally normal to ask questions of your co-workers as you make conversation. That said, it's hard to know when you've crossed the line, especially when it comes to topics about gender.

Empathy Session

Carlos invites a job candidate for an interview. To prepare for the interview, Carlos searches for the candidate online. The first result shows photos of the candidate, Katie, at her baby shower.

Question

How should Carlos handle this information about the candidate?

Facts To Know

Asking personal questions about family and personal life can open you or your business up to the risk of a lawsuit. This is especially true during the interview process.

Women with children may be seen as less committed to their careers, while the opposite is true for men with children. Co-workers are more likely to perceive women with children as irresponsible, distracted, or spread too thin. This phenomenon is referred to as the "motherhood penalty."

To learn more about the research supporting the "motherhood penalty," read "Getting a Job: Is There a Motherhood Penalty?" by Correll, Benard, and Paik.[17]

---

[17] bit.ly/2PhhVRJ

You can brief yourself on the issue by reading "The Pregnancy Penalty: How Working Women Pay for Having Kids" or "The Motherhood Penalty vs. the Fatherhood Bonus."[18,19]

Actions

Do not ask women about marital status, health, child-rearing, or family planning. Generally avoid related topics.

- A woman's family situation could negatively impact her career trajectory or her candidacy for a senior position.

- When you ask questions about the personal lives of women, or pressure them to volunteer personal information, you risk exposing them to negative bias.

- If you ask inappropriate questions, you become a liability to your employer.

---

[18] theatln.tc/2zbzbC5
[19] nyti.ms/2pPFHee

- Learn more about off-limit topics by reading the US Government's overview of "Prohibited Employment Policies/Practices."[20]

Know which words may negatively affect your co-workers. If you avoid the following words, you will have a more universally-welcoming vocabulary.

Bitch
Before you call a woman "bitch," ask if you would think negatively of a man who did the same things as this woman. You may be subconsciously averse to a woman's behavior, like speaking authoritatively, because she is a woman. If you decide this woman is worthy of name-calling, replace "bitch" with a specific description like "callous bully" or "irritable gossip."

---

[20] bit.ly/2jLoiQX

Bossy
"Bossy" is used to characterize someone who is too assertive and demanding. "Bossy" is more often used to describe women rather than men.

Hysterical
The word "hysterical" has a paternalistic history. Doctors used to diagnose women who experienced nervousness, laughter, or tears with "hysteria." In the 1800s, medical treatments for hysteria included massaging the patient's clitoris until climax. Even today, any strongly-emotive woman risks being diagnosed with hysteria.   *(continued)*

A Google Trends search for the terms "hysterical man" and "hysterical woman" demonstrates that men are rarely described as "hysterical" (see Chart 3).

HOW WE SEARCH FOR HYSTERIA

Based on Google Trends search term interest score.
The score is based on relatively popularity over time.

Chart 3. How We Search for Hysteria.

Dick, dickhead, dickwad, prick

Generally speaking, references to genitals are inappropriate. Keep penis references under wraps at work. The logical conclusion: don't tell dick jokes at work!

Ballsy, grow a pair

"Ballsy" promotes the idea that humans with balls are the only kind of humans courageous enough to take high-risk, high-reward actions. Also, the genitals rule.

Ballbuster, ball-breaker
You know the drill...no genitalia-related words.

Pussy
One more time...Repeat after me: "No. Genitalia-related. Words."

Guys
A lot of us grew up calling groups of people "guys." For example, "Hey guys, let's go..." At the same time, you could try out saying, "Hey everyone, let's go..." It can't hurt.

Sweetie, girl, honey, hon, little lady, miss

Words like "Sweetie," "girl," and "honey" are pejorative terms for women. It's unlikely that a co-worker has instructed you to call them by one of these names. You've likely never heard a co-worker say, "Please don't call me by my name, Katie. I prefer to go by Sweetie."

Fuck

The term directly refers to sexual intercourse, and as such, is inappropriate.

Thrusting, grinding, fucking, mounting
Once again, references to sexual intercourse are inappropriate.

Rape
Rarely, men casually equate rape to losing a competition. For example, "Bill got raped at his quarterly performance review." Do not use rape as a metaphor.
It's likely that someone in the office who overhears an offhand comment about rape: a) has been raped; or b) has a significant other, friend, or family member who has been raped. In 2016, the US government's Bureau of Justice

(continued)

Statistics (BJS) surveyed "a total of 134,690 households and 224,520 persons age 12 or older."[21] During that year, 1.2 of every 1000 people surveyed reported to the BJS that they had experienced rape or sexual assault. According to RAINN (Rape, Abuse & Incest National Network), "1 out of every 6 American women has been the victim of an attempted or completed rape in her lifetime (14.8% completed, 2.8% attempted)."[22]

Day-to-day, if you're wondering about a word that is not included in this list, remember:

- Avoid words that refer to genitalia or intercourse.

- Avoid words that refer to women in pejorative ways.

- Avoid adjectives which are often used to describe only women or only men.

---

[21] bit.ly/2iCUza6
[22] bit.ly/2bwskd7

- Avoid words with prolific and entertaining *Urban Dictionary* definitions.

TIP 3: AUDIT YOUR WORK ENVIRONMENT

The Challenge

The office space is a physical manifestation of the company's values. Therefore, the office should be organized, decorated, and stocked to welcome women employees and visitors.

Empathy Session

A journalist is visiting to write about Frank's company next week. As part of his diversity recruiting efforts, he wants to ensure that the office appeals to more people than the three men who work for him now.

Question

What can Frank do to ensure that his small business makes a good impression and feels welcoming to everyone?

Facts To Know

In the fall of 2017, following multiple lawsuits, Fidelity Investments made serious moves to improve its office culture. The company assigned mandatory sexual harassment training to employees and established a sexual harassment committee.

At the same time, Fidelity's CEO Abigail Johnson made a personal attempt to improve office culture by physically moving her desk. According to the *Boston Globe,* Johnson now sits in the same room as the "portfolio managers, research analysts, and traders" who faced the most "scrutiny of Fidelity's workplace conditions" following the lawsuits.[23] This move will position her—quite literally—in the right place to discover why the organization is unwelcoming to women, and how to resolve this issue.

Making the office a welcoming place for women can be even easier than moving desks. In fact, some of the

---

[23] bit.ly/2Hq83RA

smallest adjustments to physical space can have a profound effect on how women feel.

For example, designated lactation rooms make a world of difference for women who are nursing. Even if the mother elects not to breastfeed, she needs to find a private space to relieve herself by pumping milk every few hours. If you want to watch a funny video on the topic, check out "If Men Breastfed" from Naya Health.[24] The video points out how much better breastfeeding at work can be when everyone in the workplace supports the process.

"That is so funny! Yup, lactation lounges would indeed exist if men breastfed, and the workplace would look much different if men were doing the breastfeeding.

I remember that, with my third child, I had to

(continued)

---

[24] youtu.be/Rko_jlXgiy8

pump in the morning and afternoon during short 15-minute breaks. I used to cringe when I made it to our sunrise meetings at 7:30 am on time when the men would stroll in a little late. If they only knew.

Unlike most staff, I had the luxury of being able to step into a co-worker's office. I was just hoping that people could not hear the [pumping] machine grinding away. Nope, no one asked if I needed a refrigerator to keep the milk cold. I hauled in a mini cooler each day."

— Woman in Law Industry

Curious to know another set of women-specific office needs? Sometimes women menstruate at an unexpected moment, or simply forget the supplies they need. Your office supplies Kleenex for unexpected sneezes, colds, and drippy noses. Not all employees use the Kleenex, but it's common sense to have them around. Menstrual hygiene supplies belong to the same class of disposable, absorbent health products. While it might cost a bit to offer this benefit, it certainly costs less than an employee who needs to take a long break to make a trip to the drugstore.

Actions

Audit your office environment for sexual innuendo and remove it. For example, "Romance Chamber," "The Break-Up Room," and "Arrears" seem like ill-advised names for conference rooms. Do you really want to invite Martha to meet you in the "Romance Chamber" on Friday at 4pm?

Dropbox Office Design Rendering by Custom Spaces [25]

- Remove sexual art and suggestive pin-ups.

- Scan group chat lists like Slack for inappropriate language. Communicate with repeat offenders, asking them to refrain from sharing sexually-charged content.

- Ensure that the office generally excludes references to romance and relationship status.

Determine which government compliance posters you are required to post in your office.

- Visit the *"FirstStep* Poster Advisor" created by the Department of Labor (DOL) to help you

---

[25] bit.ly/2PkeutB

through the process. The site presents a series of easy questions you can answer in a few minutes.[26]

- Once you have determined your requirements, browse the DOL library of free printable posters.[27]

- Order the posters and display them where all your employees can learn from them.

Make minor improvements to the bathrooms.

- If your company has unisex toilets, leave seats down as a courtesy to the women in the office.

- Consider supplying toilet seat covers. You'll want to look for disposable toilet seat covers and a complementary toilet seat cover dispenser. Example Product: http://amzn.to/2HS6T0B.

- Ensure that bathrooms have a lined trash can. Empty this trash can at least once a week.

---

[26] bit.ly/2aysMpB
[27] bit.ly/2BaHnQF

Stock menstrual hygiene products in the bathroom.

- Buy underwear liners. Look for individually wrapped, unscented panty-liners. Example product: http://amzn.to/2Ht8f2A.

- Buy tampons. Look for individually wrapped, unscented tampons for "regular flow." Example product: http://amzn.to/2BDn55V.

- Buy sanitary disposal bags to help with disposal of used feminine hygiene products. Without sanitary disposal bags, women might resort to flushing the used products down the toilet, which may impact plumbing. Example product: http://amzn.to/2EDVJjb.

If expectant or nursing mothers work in your office, make a plan for how you can help them manage their breastfeeding routine.

- Provide refrigerator space that is dedicated to storing milk.

- Allocate a private space for pumping.

Introduce women influencers to the office.

- If you have books in the office, check to see how many of those books are written by men. See if you can flesh out your collection with more books written by women.

- If you regularly host speakers, audit your upcoming agenda. Of the speakers who visit, how many are women, and how many are men?

Formalize internal programs and opportunities for women employees.

- Establish a mentorship program. Pair junior employees at your company with more senior employees.

- Start a recurring event for women. For example, you could start a book club, or hold a recurring monthly lunch.

- Assign both men *and* women on your team challenging projects that push them to develop their potential.

- Keep a record of the promotions offered to men and women at similar stages of their career. If you notice an imbalance, make a plan to correct course.

TIP 4: LEARN TO LISTEN FULLY

The Challenge

Studies have shown that women are more likely to be interrupted while speaking than men. When this happens repeatedly, women cannot voice their opinions and may stop taking initiative to contribute to the conversation.

Empathy Session

Mike met with Ruby and Jim on Thursday about a joint project to increase sales. On Friday morning, Mike recalls that, in this meeting, Ruby offered only a few ideas and spoke very little.

Question

How could Mike have noticed that he and Jim dominated the conversation, even before the meeting was over? How could Mike have signaled to Ruby that he valued her input from the start?

Facts To Know

In 1975, Don H. Zimmerman and Candace West investigated how interruption patterns might vary by gender. They found "striking asymmetries between men and women with respect to patterns of interruption, silence, and support for partner in the development of topics." They concluded that "males assert an asymmetrical right to control topics and do so without evident repercussions."[28]

In other words, Zimmerman and West found that men were much freer to speak persistently without being cut off. Other researchers, like Adrienne Hancock and Benjamin Rubin, have come to similar conclusions, finding "when speaking with a female, participants [of either gender] interrupted more and used more dependent clauses than when speaking with a male."[29] Meaning that both men and women are guilty of interrupting women at a higher rate than they interrupt men.

---

[28] bit.ly/2Fn5hhH
[29] bit.ly/2la3teI

Even outside of academic circles men have a certain reputation for dominating conversation by cutting women off. In popular culture, women have come up with their own word for describing this phenomenon: "manterrupting."

"1. Always give full attention and listen whenever a female member in a male-dominated meeting speaks/shares her thoughts.

2. Push female members in my projects or teams I lead, to be the lead speaker whenever possible and also get recognition for their work."

— Male Technology Strategist

"I worked in the high tech sector as a mechanical engineer. I worked closely with another female engineer who was a little less experienced, and I took her under my wing. Because I wanted to be an advocate, I had explicit conversations with her about how she felt her gender affected her interactions in this environment.

She stated she didn't feel like she was heard as easily as the men and that her ideas were often times not given the same credence as her male counterparts. There are some confounding factors in this, but I kept watch thereafter and it was generally true.

I noticed male colleagues would unintentionally talk over her and I, being unfortunately brazen, would say "Hold on, what did you say?" to bring the conversation back into her hands.

(continued)

Listen before you talk, give space after someone finishes their sentence. This should be applied to all interactions, but I find that as a male I have the privilege of dominating a conversation. So that means I have the responsibility to ensure everyone is a member of the conversation."

— Male Mechanical Engineer

Actions

Self-educate and learn what it's like to be a woman who frequently gets interrupted at work.

- Read Dr. Kieran Snyder's article "How To Get Ahead As A Woman In Tech: Interrupt Men" to understand the interruption dynamic.[30] Dr. Snyder diligently tracked the number of times men and women were interrupted at her workplace.

---

[30] slate.me/1kVarx3

Self-evaluate your own habit of interrupting in general.

- Next time you are in a meeting, when you think that it's your turn to talk, count to seven before speaking.
- Practice "active listening": repeat key phrases and summarize others' ideas to ensure that you understand what others are saying before moving onto your point.

Self-evaluate your own habit of interrupting women.

- Do you cut women off while they are talking?
- Notice and correct your behavior.

Facilitate egalitarian conversation.

- Take note of the number of men and women who speak at meetings, at events, and in public forums.
- If you find that fewer women than men are speaking, identify opportunities for women to speak to the entire team, company, and community.

- If you notice that one individual in a group meeting disengages, look for ways to include them in the conversation.

- All team members may not enjoy public speaking; provide other avenues for sharing research, work, and opinions. For example, introverted co-workers might prefer to write an article rather than give a presentation.

TIP 5: IMPROVE PSYCHOLOGICAL SAFETY

The Challenge

Research shows that the most productive teams are those comprised of people who trust and respect one another. To build such trust within a team, make co-workers feel good by acknowledging their feelings and contributions.

Empathy Session

For weeks, Jake, Rachel, Jenny, and Chloe work together to solve a difficult business problem. They contribute equally to the project, building off of each others' work. After they solve the problem, Jake gives an important presentation regarding the outcome to the entire company, which is well-received. However, Jake does not directly credit Rachel, Jenny, or Chloe with their contributions to the project.

Question

How does Jake's failure to credit his three teammates impact the team going forward? Now that this has happened, how can Jake work to rebuild trust?

Facts To Know

Google's "Project Aristotle," rumored to have cost millions of dollars, investigated why certain teams work better than others. The project's main finding was straightforward: teammates who feel "psychologically safe" make more successful teams.[31] To build a psychologically safe team, all teammates must feel secure enough to admit mistakes, innovate beyond norms, and expose themselves to social vulnerability.

Watch "Building A Psychologically Safe Workplace" with Amy Edmondson, which explains why people

---

[31] nyti.ms/2jAq4mD

fear taking social risks at work and how to reduce that fear.[32]

In recent years, women have created slang to describe ways that men threaten their psychological safety at work. "Mansplaining" happens when a man explains something (often patently obvious) to a woman in a pompous tone. Mash together "bro" and "appropriating," and you'll get "bropropriating," which describes a situation where a man credits himself for a woman's idea. In the fall of 2017, astronomer Nicole Gugliucci popularized the term "hepeat" with a tweet that went viral. In her tweet, Nicole explains that the word combines "he" and "repeat," referring to the phenomenon where "a woman suggests an idea and it's ignored, but then a guy says [the] same thing and everyone loves it."[33] This type of specialized vocabulary clearly resonates with women's collective experience: the concept of "hepeat" earned Gugliucci 206,000 Likes and 67,000 Retweets by June 2018.

---

[32] youtu.be/LhoLuui9gX8
[33] bit.ly/2K3aE8o

Actions

Get better at recognizing the feelings and needs of others.

- Watch your co-workers' expressions and body language for clues about how they are feeling.

- To get better at reading body language, read Kendra Cherry's article "Understanding Body Language and Facial Expressions."[34]

- Take note of where your co-workers situate themselves physically. You might notice that colleagues, especially women, seek privacy in stairwells, cars, or bathroom stalls to hide their feelings.

- If you notice your co-worker is distressed, don't be shy to ask:
  - "How do you feel?"
  - "What's going on?"
  - "Can I do anything to support you?"

---

[34] bit.ly/2wRqM60

Go out of your way to make each individual co-worker feel appreciated. Taking a few minutes to thank your co-worker can be more productive than if you were to use that same time on your own project.

- Pause and give genuine, spontaneous compliments to your co-workers when they do great work. For example, you could say, "Wow. I felt [*feeling*] to see that you are so talented at [*skill*]." Or keep it simple: "You have such a knack for making spreadsheets!"

- Encourage team members to share diverse thinking and ideas. If you hear a fresh, new idea, seek to understand the new idea, rather than defaulting to judgement or defensiveness. Try responding to unfamiliar ideas with phrases like "Yes, and…" rather than "No…." or "But…"

Acknowledge your co-workers' contributions and give credit where it is due. This will help you avoid "hepeat" moments.

- If you reiterate a woman's idea, make sure to credit her as you speak.

- For example, if a woman named Amanda suggests that everyone plan an outing to the Science Museum, and you like that idea and want to circle back to it, just say, "Like Amanda said, I think we should go to the Science Museum."

- Even better, you could redirect attention back to Amanda, so she has a chance to speak for herself. Just say, "Amanda, I like your idea to go to the Science Museum. Could you tell us more?"

Make a special effort to show your appreciation of a co-worker.

- For ideas on how to show appreciation, refer to relationship expert Gary Chapman's "The Five Love Languages." In this book, he proposes that people show their appreciation for one another through five means: gift giving, quality time, words of affirmation, acts of service, and physical touch. (His work was initially geared towards romantic relationships, so as you use his advice, make sure to keep things safe-for-work.) Below I have outlined platonic ways to show appreciation to a co-worker that pay homage to Chapman's framework.

Gift Giving
<ul><li>Gift educational books to your co-worker.</li><li>Surprise your co-worker with a card.</li></ul>

Quality Time
<ul><li>Schedule regular meeting to catch up.</li><li>Invite your co-worker to lunch.</li><li>Stop by your co-worker's desk to say hello.</li></ul>

Words of Affirmation

- Write an email to thank your co-worker for what they do.
- Publicly praise your co-worker's work.
- Post a lavish LinkedIn recommendation.

Acts of Service

- Offer to give your feedback on your co-worker's project, using your unique skills to add to the project.
- Volunteer to run an errand for your co-worker, like mailing a package or getting coffee.

Physical Touch

- Make sure to limit physical touch to corporate-appropriate rituals.
- Operate under the assumption that hugs, touches to the back or shoulders, and cheek kisses are not business norms.
- Give your co-worker a strong handshake!

If you're unsure which kind of appreciation a person likes to receive, just look at how they show appreciation for others.

TIP 6: EASILY NAVIGATE CONFLICT

The Challenge

Directly resolving interpersonal disagreement with co-workers can feel intimidating. Utilize standardized conversation frameworks, written by experts, to make conflict resolution more approachable.

Empathy Session

A co-worker calls Maria a "bossy lady" to her face at a major presentation in front of senior leadership. Everyone in the room laughs. Maria is devastated, especially because a colleague who she considers a close friend, Rob, joined in on the laughter.

Question

How can Rob acknowledge the situation and repair his working relationship with Maria, even before the meeting concludes?

Facts To Know

When in an awkward or upsetting situation, it can be hard to get your thoughts straight, much less communicate how you feel. That's why there are entire organizations, books, and speaking industries devoted to teaching people how to communicate and resolve conflict more effectively.

The Center For Nonviolent Communication (CNVC) is one of these organizations.[35] The CNVC is devoted to educating people about conflict resolution methods. The center emphasizes the value of personal feelings and effective communication. More specifically, the CNVC teaches "nonviolent communication," a conflict resolution framework which they refer to as "NVC."

The NVC framework asks that you pair your *feelings* with *observation* of interpersonal dynamics or events. Next, you identify a *basic human need* that the *event observation* does not meet. Next, you make a *request* of

---

[35] cnvc.org

those directly involved in the *event observation*.
Critically, the *event observation* is described in objective
terms, without negative adjectives.

In practice, the framework sounds like this: "I felt
[*feeling*] when you [*event*]. I have a [*basic human need*].
Would you consider [*request*]?

Candor, Inc. offers an even simpler framework for
providing feedback: 1) care personally ("give a damn
about the person") and 2) challenge directly (be
"willing to piss people off" in the pursuit of offering
clarity "about what's going wrong, and what's going
right"). To learn more, you can read a description of
Kim Scott's feedback philosophy in "Radical Candor
— The Surprising Secret to Being a Good Boss."[36]

No matter the framework, give yourself time to learn
how to apply the techniques. Experts say that it takes
about three weeks to form a new habit. For a daily
habit, that's at least 21 days you can give yourself to
apply conflict resolution techniques successfully.

---

[36] bit.ly/1P7xEgf

Actions

Diversify the vocabulary you use to describe your feelings.

- The more specific your vocabulary, the easier it is for others to understand where you are coming from, and the severity of the issue. Rather than feeling "angry," perhaps you are "furious" or "livid" or even "resentful."

- If you are coming up short on feelings vocabulary, study the CNVC's curated list of "feelings we may have when our needs are being met and feelings we may have when our needs are not being met."[37]

Try to identify the motivation (or lack of motivation) of an argument.

- Internalize the fact that the goal of an argument isn't to *win*, it's to *resolve*.

- There are those who like to argue for the sake of arguing. They like to play the devil's

---

[37] bit.ly/2BQYDOL

advocate. Others in the room might feel upset or frustrated when their co-worker adopts an argumentative, sarcastic attitude.

- You can try to quell arguments by refusing to take the bait. Try asking questions like, "What is the root of this disagreement?"

- If you listen closely, you'll find that most of your co-workers argue because they care, not because they want to annoy you. Humans who argue at meetings are engaged with the team and care about the company's success. Tolerate different opinions—healthy dialogue includes divisive dialogue.

- Watch out for people who once argued and were very involved in team discussions, and who drop out suddenly, as they may have disengaged from the team or the company mission.

Resolve small conflicts before they escalate into big conflicts.

- As is feasible, identify and communicate about problems in a timely manner. For example, you could write down what happened and get your thoughts straight. Then the next day speak with whoever you had a conflict with.

- Directly contact the person who has caused distress, rather than talk about them with others, especially for the first time you have had a conflict with this person.

Practice using a conflict resolution framework, which provides a comfortingly strict structure for conflict resolution.

- Study the NVC Framework described in the "Facts To Know" section of this chapter.

- For example, you might tell a colleague: "I noticed that you have marked your calendar as "Busy" at the time we used to have a weekly meeting. I'm feeling rejected, because I look forward to that meeting as a time to connect with you. I really value this time together. Would you be willing to find another regular opportunity for us to connect?"

- Or, perhaps: "I noticed that you schedule our meetings at 4pm. I'm feeling as though my preferences are being ignored, because I've let you know that I reserve 4:30pm for planning the upcoming workday. Could you please find an alternate time?" While this approach is clunky, and almost unbearably straightforward, it definitely beats feeling a fiery rage every time your co-worker sends you a 4pm meeting invite, and exacerbating the situation every time you decline it with no explanation.

TIP 7: PROMOTE CONSCIENTIOUS DIALOGUE

The Challenge

Employee's words (including in-office banter, email threads, and chat logs) directly impact a company's culture. Employees should hold themselves accountable to using phrases that demonstrate respect for women.

Empathy Session

Andy complains that no one in the sales department ever helps him with his projects. Wendy volunteers that the department has helped her with projects in the past. Andy replies, "Oh, those sales guys just help you out because you're a girl."

Question

How should others in the room acknowledge and respond to Andy's comment?

Facts To Know

Microaggressions are the little things people say or do that make members of a specific minority group feel uncomfortable. A microaggression might disguise itself as a joke or a subtle difference in behavior. For example, a supervisor might train the people on his team differently: he might advise the women to maintain a cheerful facial expression and ask nicely for help; and, he might advise the men to speak assertively and take risks.

Acknowledge the microaggressions you hear as they emerge in conversation, because it's unlikely that they will get reported after the fact. The target of a microaggression may think the incident is not significant enough to warrant reporting. Or, she may fear risking her professional reputation by reporting an event that might be dismissed later because "he didn't mean it that way."

Even if you are in a group, do not wait for a signal from others before speaking up. The group setting can dilute one's individual sense of responsibility, making members of the group less likely to speak up. In psychology this phenomenon is known as the "bystander effect."

"A guy came into my office to pitch. He's in his mid-50s. He brought with him a late-20s, early 30s engineer, who happened to be a woman. The other guy in the room was an ex-collegiate football player.

The first guy proceeded to make two to three specific comments, making fun of this woman's appearance and weight. The first comment was about lunch. He said, 'You're more of a salad kind of girl, right?' She said she likes steak. Then he said, 'Yeah I know.' Then we felt uncomfortable. But she looked okay, so we kept talking.

It comes up that the engineer is going on

(continued)

vacation. Then he points to the engineer and says that she's pale, skinny, and gross. He says that it's lucky she's going on vacation to get a tan.

The first joke I laughed once, because I was surprised. The second joke I was silent, and watched the two guys giggle with each other. She did not talk the entire time.

This guy was making asinine comments about her appearance and weight. He was obviously trying to connect with me as a 'dude.'

I thought about telling them, 'I thought about using your company, but you're an asshole to women.' I thought about writing to the guys who set up the meeting, and telling them. I thought about reaching out to her, but I'm worried it won't help, because the office

(continued)

obviously has an environment that's not nice to women.

They were obviously trying to bond. He obviously doesn't understand the sensitivities of the industry. Making a joke to venture capitalists about women is not allowed. Not only is it not cool, but he obviously doesn't understand what's going on in the Valley right now. The zeitgeist in the Valley is very much that, if that is who you are, you're not getting anywhere.

They are assholes. But how many dollars is it worth? It's a very tenuous thing. This guy is a representative of a much larger system. It's like a broader business ethics question. Do you end the business relationship on the basis of one meeting?
Eventually I wrote my boss an email. I told him about the situation, and my boss wrote

(continued)

back that we only need to work with people who are honorable."

— Male Venture Capital Investor

Actions

Learn how to recognize unwelcoming comments as they happen.

- Remember, a negative comment is not always an angry outburst or a direct insult. It often disguises itself as "just a joke."
- During my research, women shared unwelcoming phrases that had been used in their presence. Learn from these examples:
  - One man said that work was "busting [his] balls."
  - Another man said that a project "raped [him]."
  - Another man said that a task "had [him] bent over."

- And yet another told a woman to "just man up."
- Finally, one woman overheard a male colleague declare, "That project needed a coat-hanger abortion."

When you see or hear someone acting in an unwelcoming way, stand up for what's right and take action to resolve the situation.

- If you hear an upsetting remark, pause for a moment. Give people a chance to reflect on their word choice, so that they have the opportunity to rephrase their statement.
- Counter a co-worker's off-color remark by repeating his words back to him, and asking why. For example, "Hey, I just heard you say 'That project raped me.' Why did you say that?"
- If you're feeling bold, say "Hey man, that's not cool. I don't think it's appropriate to talk that way."
- Or you can say, "I think the way you're talking is disrespectful."

Don't wait for others to speak up about an inappropriate comment or behavior.

- Trust your intuition.
- Beware of these common pitfalls:
    - Assuming: "She hasn't said anything, so she's probably not upset."
    - Justifying: "It's just a personality quirk of that one guy. He always makes jokes like that."
- You may notice others signaling their discomfort with body language, rather than words; they may avoid eye contact with you or cross their arms.
- The more you call out inappropriate moments for what they are, the more confident you'll feel.

TIP 8: ENCOURAGE COMMUNITY WELL-BEING

The Challenge

Healthy employees bring the best version of themselves to work. Make healthy lifestyle choices: your health will improve and you may inspire your co-workers to make healthy changes of their own.

Empathy Session

Evan works at a company that caters lunch every day. An amazing benefit! He starts work at 7:30 AM. At 11:30 AM, he grabs lunch from the kitchen, then continues working at his desk. Before he knows it, it's 7:00 PM and the sun has set. Recently Evan realizes that he does not leave the office, and wants to start going for a walk each afternoon. However, he hesitates to do so because all of his co-workers stay inside during the day, too.

Question

Why do you think Evan's company decided to cater lunch for its employees? How can Evan create a healthy routine?

Facts To Know

In the long run, a healthy workplace is a more profitable and productive workplace. Employees will take fewer sick days, make sharper decisions, stay more engaged at work, and avoid burnout. To educate yourself on the significant business benefits of a healthy workforce, read *Harvard Business Review*'s article "What's the Hard Return on Employee Wellness Programs?"[38]

An integral, yet frequently overlooked component of employee wellness is allowing employees time to fulfill personal caretaking responsibilities outside of work. Just as employees must show up for work, they must also show up for their loved ones.

---

[38] bit.ly/2nZJnte

Importantly, when a workplace fails to help employees fulfill commitments at home, it affects women more than men. In 2015, the Pew Research Center found "four-in-ten working mothers (42%) say that at some point in their working life, they had reduced their hours in order to care for a child or other family member, while just 28% of working fathers say they had done the same."[39] In the same group surveyed, women were three times more likely than men to say that they left their career because of family obligations.

Finally, the government has labor laws in place to ensure employees are protected should they absolutely need to prioritize family health over their jobs. The Family and Medical Leave Act (FMLA) ensures that employees can take leave for major family care events like: newborn in need of care, newly adopted child in need of care, or a family member in need of care because of a serious medical condition. The act applies to companies with 50 or

---

[39] pewrsr.ch/1AcL8wN

more employees. Additionally, many states have similar laws and programs in place.

Actions

Model healthy behavior for your team, whether you are the founder or the newest addition of the company.

- Make time to eat meals.
- Take breaks from sitting at your desk.
- Take walks outside, or exercise during the day.
- Stay hydrated. Water and herbal tea are great alternatives to coffee and beer.
- If you are sick, work or rest from home rather than exposing others to your illness.

Advocate for company events and practices that welcome the entire team.

- Minimize evening activities. This simple scheduling change will boost the number of employees that can attend events, especially for those with family obligations. Instead of a night at the bar, try daytime games, meals, or group walks during work hours.

- Plan activities with an alcohol-free component so that everyone can fully participate. Events that don't pressure employees to drink alcohol will foster a feeling of inclusion across your team, especially for employees who have private health concerns.

Help employees fulfill caretaking commitments to family and loved ones.

- Experiment with offering flexible work hours.

- Consider making a subset of the work day mandatory to facilitate meetings and team culture. Allow the remaining hours to be set flexibly by individual employees who consistently perform and deliver results.

- Make FMLA policy publicly available in your office and on your company's internal documents, as well as the company blog. Publish your company's family leave policy, as well as the paternity and maternity leave policy. If you aren't in a position to write this policy yourself, request that leadership do so. If you don't want to bring attention to yourself, you can say that you are inquiring for recruiting purposes.

TIP 9: MAINTAIN APPROPRIATE INTIMACY

The Challenge

Good men may fear unintentionally getting a reputation for making women uncomfortable. To avoid this reputation, consistently welcome women by establishing clear personal-professional boundaries and acting appropriately.

Empathy Session

At Katie's annual work review, her supervisor Bill reports on her exemplary productivity and collaborative attitude. Bill asks how satisfied she is with the workplace culture, especially as the only woman on the team. Katie says, "Is it good? No one is touching me, so yeah it's good..." She confides that at previous jobs, co-workers touched her shoulder, waist, or knee on a daily basis. She's simply relieved to work on a team where no one touches her inappropriately.

Question

Why do you think Katie mentioned this work history? How might Bill follow up to ensure that Katie is treated appropriately in other ways beyond touching?

Facts To Know

An employee can inadvertently leverage power over a subordinate. This can happen when senior employees think that their subordinates have the ability to opt out of potentially uncomfortable requests. However, subordinate employees often cannot practically exercise this right, as their job depends on their supervisor's approval.

For example, imagine a senior employee asks a junior employee on a date to the movies during business hours. The junior employee must consider that denying the invitation could embarrass or upset her boss, and perhaps result in her being fired. Rather than say no, the junior employee might say yes, because it would require her to take on significant professional and financial risk to disagree.

On the other hand, some men worry their intentions may be misinterpreted as inappropriate and avoid professional relationships with women entirely. Leaders must not shy away from mentorship positions, fearing liability. This avoidant behavior robs women of valuable mentorship from men, and the ability to participate equally at work. Mentors provide critical support for young employees as they establish their careers.

Actions

Act in an appropriate manner given your level of influence at work. You may hold undue influence over an employee, given that their livelihood and reputation depends on your satisfaction with their performance.

- Understand if you might have influence over your co-workers. Employees who likely have seniority over others hold titles like: Owner, Founder, CEO, Manager, Supervisor, or Lead.

- As a senior employee, do not ask junior employees to complete non-job-related tasks or favors (e.g., asking an employee to give you a massage).

- As a senior employee, plan events that do not revolve around sexually explicit themes. For example, do not book a company retreat and transport employees on a bus outfitted with a stripper pole. (Yes, this really happened to one of the engineers who was interviewed. Her employer booked a bus filled with loud music, stocked with beer, and outfitted with a stripper pole in the center. The multi-hour drive further disintegrated as her drunk boss started thrusting at the pole.)

Learn how to recognize generally inappropriate behavior, as well as potential workplace harassment.

- Frequent touching, sexual or physical jokes or comments, and unwarranted judgement about a colleague's romantic choices or habits *absolutely* cross a boundary.

- The US Department of Labor (DOL) formally describes two types of harassment. Type One harassment is called *"Quid Pro Quo* Harassment." Type Two harassment is called "Hostile Work Environment Harassment."

- *"Quid Pro Quo* Harassment" can make an employee feel like she must complete a sexual act *in exchange* for keeping her job. A DOL example of this harassment is a "supervisor who fires or denies promotion to a subordinate for refusing to be sexually cooperative."

- "Hostile Work Environment Harassment" occurs when an employee or employees persistently behave in such a way (sexually, crudely, or otherwise) that the workplace culture and environment feels hostile. A DOL example of this harassment is "telling off-color jokes concerning race, sex, disability, or other protected bases."

- For more details, read "What do I need to know about...WORKPLACE HARASSMENT," the DOL's outline of Federal harassment policy.[40]

Establish a structure to report harassment up the chain of command.

- If you are in a position to develop a harassment reporting structure, create one now.

- If you cannot personally develop a harassment reporting policy, then ask HR, or the business owner, to create one.

- If you observe a senior employee harassing a junior employee, step up. Do your best to state clearly, and in-the-moment, that the senior employee is acting inappropriately. If you can't bring yourself to speak up as it happens, take the initiative to write an account of the event or reach out to HR with a concern.

---

[40] bit.ly/2wjYkb1

- To review the government's harassment reporting laws, visit the US Equal Employment Opportunity Commission's website.[41]

Create mentorship opportunities, both informal and formal, to increase the number of positive interactions women have with men at work.

- If you have relevant experience, make yourself available to answer general operational questions (e.g., how to grab a great parking spot) and bigger career questions (e.g., how to negotiate for a raise).
- If you have a specific area of expertise, offer guidance to junior employees as they tackle challenging projects.
- Treat your mentees equally regardless of their gender. If you like to invite mentees for coffee or drinks, make sure to invite women just as often as you invite men.

---

[41] bit.ly/2mwoxxL

Establish strong and healthy romantic boundaries.

- As a rule, do not engage in intimacy that goes beyond the need to perform your job.

- You have heard this advice before—*don't* get into the romance game at work.

- If you insist on romantically involving yourself with a co-worker, make sure you have her ongoing, enthusiastic consent.

- Additionally, read up on your workplace's written workplace romantic relationship policy.

- If you are in a leadership position, formalize a written workplace romantic relationship policy.

TIP 10: PREPARE TO APOLOGIZE

The Challenge

Despite our best intentions, we all make mistakes at work. How we react to these mistakes shapes our workplace culture. Recognize mistakes when you make them and apologize in earnest.

Empathy Session

Charlie spots a fresh bouquet on Amy's desk. As Amy opens the card, Charlie asks, "Do you have a boyfriend?" Amy does not respond and looks away with a frown. Charlie realizes that his comment may have made Amy feel uncomfortable.

Question

How might Charlie follow up with Amy to evaluate if an apology is necessary? If an apology is in order, how should he go about making amends?

Facts To Know

A proper apology should not include an excuse. It's not hard to find others who agree with this statement.

- Benjamin Franklin, polymath and Founding Father, said: "He that is good for making excuses is seldom good for anything else."

- Florence Nightingale, statistician and nurse, noted, "I attribute my success to this: I never gave or took an excuse."

- Kimberly Johnson, poet and Guggenheim Fellow, said, "Never ruin an apology with an excuse."

That said, this kind of advice is easy to give, but hard to live. In the next section, we'll provide practical steps for how to make an excuse-free apology.

Actions

Learn from your mistakes through self reflection. Write out answers to the following questions:

- "What was my mistake? What actions did I take and how did I behave?"
- "How did my attitude contribute to this mistake?"
- "How might I avoid repeating this mistake in the future? What specific actions can I take now to improve myself?"

Recognize whether you owe someone an earnest apology. Listed below are some indications that you may need to apologize.

- You feel remorse or regret because of an action that does not match your self-image.
- You said something to a co-worker that could undermine mutual trust or a productive working relationship.
- Someone told you that you have hurt their feelings, or someone else's feelings.

When you make an apology, incorporate the following elements:

- Accept that you are responsible. If you are making an apology, then you did something wrong.
- Make your apology in a private space. Look for a conference room, grab a coffee, or take a walk.
- Apologize in a timely manner.
- Propose your plan to prevent making the same mistake in the future.

When you make an apology, avoid these common pitfalls:

- Don't tell others how they should have felt. You are not a mind reader.
- Don't shift the blame from yourself.
- Don't justify, defend, or dismiss your actions.

CONCLUSION

Congratulations! You've finished reading "Don't Tell Dick Jokes at Work (and Other Tips)," which is an important first step toward improving the workplace for women.

You're better prepared to foster a safe workplace for women. You will notice and understand, in a richer sense, workplace interactions that might alienate women co-workers.

Think back to the beginning of this book, when you read statements and advice from women like:

- "I am equal, capable, and strong."
- "I am not 'aggressive' or 'sensitive' or 'controlling.'"
- "A company should have a professional atmosphere. Act professionally around women, as well as around men."
- "Speak professionally, without profanities or sexual innuendos."

- "Consider whether your actions contribute to the organization's goals."

Now you can recognize context behind their comments because you know *why* to foster a safe workplace for women and *how* to do so. Furthermore, you can share this knowledge with your co-workers.

NEXT STEPS

Join the Newsletter

Stay Motivated by subscribing to the FREE Quarterly Newsletter "Just The Tips!"

- Receive hot new tips for how to welcome women at work.
- Get fresh news highlights and curated reading recommendations.
- Sign up now at: www.juliadavids.com/book-subscription.

Enlighten a Co-Worker

Buy a copy of "Don't Tell Dick Jokes At Work (And Other Helpful Tips)" for a friend or co-worker here: https://bit.ly/2tPVD0c.

Spread the word on LinkedIn:

- Men, what have you done to help your women colleagues feel more welcome at work? Not sure? Read "Don't Tell Dick Jokes at Work (and Other Tips)" at https://bit.ly/2tPVD0c!

- Calling all gentlemen. Read the book that will teach you how to feel professional and confident around women at work. https://bit.ly/2tPVD0c

Write a Review

- Write a Review for this book on Amazon: https://www.amazon.com/review/create-review?asin=B07F7RNGKH#. I do hope you enjoyed reading the book and found it useful in your own life!

Contact the Author

This book is an independent publication. The author welcomes advice for how to improve the book via email.

- Send feedback to talkhumantome@gmail.com.